Columbia University

Contributions to Education

Teachers College Series

No. 666

AMS PRESS

NEW YORK

Analysis of Completion Sentences and Arithmetical Problems as Items for Intelligence Tests

By

HENRY DANIEL RINSLAND, Ph.D.

Professor of School Measurements
University of Oklahoma

TEACHERS COLLEGE, COLUMBIA UNIVERSITY
CONTRIBUTIONS TO EDUCATION, NO. 666

Bureau of Publications
Teachers College, Columbia University
NEW YORK CITY
1935

Library of Congress Cataloging in Publication Data

Rinsland, Henry Daniel, 1889–
    Analysis of completion sentences and arithmetical
problems as items for intelligence tests.

    Reprint of the 1935 ed., issued in series: Teachers
College, Columbia University. Contributions to edu-
cation, no. 666.
    Originally presented as the author's thesis, Columbia.
    Bibliography: p.
    1. Mental tests. I. Title. II. Series: Columbia
University. Teachers College. Contributions to edu-
cation, no. 666.
LB1131.R55 1972   153.9'3   73-177192
ISBN 0-404-55666-3

Reprinted by Special Arrangement with Teachers
College Press, New York, New York

From the edition of 1935, New York
First AMS edition published in 1972
Manufactured in the United States

AMS PRESS, INC.
NEW YORK, N. Y.   10003

ACKNOWLEDGMENTS

To PROFESSOR EDWARD L. THORNDIKE I owe much for his generous encouragement which has stimulated and enabled me to continue my graduate study and to attempt an investigation in a field in which he has worked. I am deeply grateful for the use of materials developed by him which have made possible this study. I especially appreciate the suggestions made by Dr. Ralph B. Spence, Dr. Helen M. Walker, and Dr. Rudolf Pintner, of Teachers College, Columbia University.

H. D. R.

CONTENTS

ANALYSIS OF COMPLETION SENTENCES AND ARITHMETICAL PROBLEMS AS ITEMS FOR INTELLIGENCE TESTS

CHAPTER I

THE PROBLEM AND ITS HISTORY

THE history of mental measurements is filled with the use of the completion form of test ever since the earliest efforts of Ebbinghaus [1897] when he published a new method for testing the mental capacity of school children at the behest of the aldermen of Breslau. Another form of test, widely used in later intelligence testing, is problem solving in arithmetic. These two forms of tests are included in the well-known CAVD Intelligence Tests by Thorndike ['26]. The fact that there is a wide use of these two forms; the fact that arithmetical problem solving is taught directly, at least in part, in school, and completion is not taught as such in school; the fact that there is in the literature of intelligence testing the question of the choice of novel tasks or the choice of commonly taught tasks; and the fact that completion and problem solving make up exactly one-half of the items at each level of the CAVD Intelligence Test, make any serious investigation of these forms valuable to the advancement of mental measurement.

Since the publication of the CAVD tests and the preliminary studies concerned with their standardization, there have been little reported data of their use and their relationships with other measures. Clark ['25] reported correlations of CAVD with several general intelligence tests (these are included and discussed by Thorndike in *The Measurement of Intelligence* ['26]. Holzinger ['31], using these correlations, claims that "Thorndike's C.A.V.D. is full of G." Hunsicker used the completion and arithmetical problem items, ". . . to measure the relation between rate of performance and level of ability in that performance." ['25, p. 15.] Garrett correlated "total scores," not altitude scores, in CAVD with college

1

grades in English, social science, classics, mathematics, and modern language ['30, p. 104]. Lorge, in order to determine whether his groups should be equated, correlated CAVD with the initial scores of subjects on the stabilimeter, mirror reading, nonsense numbers, and code substitution ['30, p. 53]. He also reported a correlation between CAVD level scores and a general examination required of candidates for degrees at Teachers College [p. 53].

The general plan of learning experiments, in which subjects practice for a number of days on tasks, lends itself to a study of the CAVD items. If under such general conditions as are controlled by these learning experiments, certain well-known characteristics of intelligence are discovered, we have further evidence of what CAVD items measure. It is the purpose of this study to analyze the completion and problem solving items in the CAVD tests by use of the general plan of learning experiments.

One of the earliest descriptions of a learning experiment using the practice exercise was given by Binet [1899]. His findings were attacked by Spearman and Krueger ['07], who used data gathered by Oehrn in 1899. Since 1908 Thorndike and his students have examined many phases of the problem. Five studies in this field by Race ['22], Kincaid ['25], Ruch ['25], Wilson ['28], and A. I. Gates ['28], present the important experiments up to the date of each investigation and additional data of important nature. They discuss the theoretical principles involved in such a way that it is unnecessary to review here what they have done, except to point out the procedures which are used in this study and the particular items which determine the departures of the present experiment from those mentioned and conducted by previous writers. Many other experiments using the practice exercise plan in learning have been reported, but the ones mentioned above give sufficient illustrations to show the plan adopted for the present study.

There is no need of harmonizing learning experiments using

mental tasks of such widely varying natures and contents as were those used in the studies mentioned above. An examination of these studies seems to indicate the following: first, that there is probably no general ability or capacity to learn which exists in any large amount common to learnings that vary from the lowest physical aspects of sensory-motor functions to the most complicated and difficult abstract functions; second, that some types of learning are more closely related than other types to the intelligence measured by intelligence tests.

However, some of the differences in findings have been due to errors in the statistical units used in defining improvement. Chapman ['25] claims that Reed's ['24] error is in taking ratios of factors with unknown zeros. Peterson ['24], reviewing Johnson's ['23] data, takes the time curves instead of the attainment curves which Johnson uses and finds just the opposite from Johnson's conclusions.

Two general characteristics which are common to practically all the experiments mentioned above, and all those reviewed by Race, Kincaid, Ruch, and Wilson, have been instrumental in determining the writer's approach to the problem. First, these earlier experiments used mental tasks in which subjects were to learn merely more of the same thing or to learn to do the same thing faster, better, or with less error—that is, improvement is defined by the ability to learn the same thing faster or better rather than to learn different content within the same function in a given order of difficulty. Nowhere do we have materials used that change from task to task, or tasks that are arranged in increasing order of difficulty, or tasks of the distinct type commonly used in intelligence tests such as sentence completion and arithmetic problem solving. The use of simple material for learning tasks is questioned by Stoddard ['25] in reviewing the evidence presented by Kincaid. Stoddard is of the opinion that none of the experiments of the type Kincaid studied can be accepted at face value or apply in the higher realms of learning. If the tasks used are of different content more complicated and abstract, and are arranged in a definite order of difficulty, we may have another method of describing intelligence. The second common characteristic is an error in the units of measurement by which the improvement is determined. The units of measurement have not been based on an approximate zero as in handwriting, drawing, and sewing scales or on an absolute zero, which is most nearly approached by certain of the measuring instruments used in physics. Thorndike, as early as 1904, pointed out the effect and need of a zero point on a scale in our measurements, but not until 1926 did he publish the first scale with an absolute zero. Chapman's ['25] criticism of statistical interpretations made on units of measures not based on zero is valid in any accurate study where things are to be compared or where there are differences, changes, and relations. If we can find tasks of a complex or pure intellectual nature which have numerical values based on an absolute zero, and these are used by subjects in the practice exercise form designed by previous experimenters in many learning experiments, we may have found another and perhaps highly accurate description of intelligence.

The importance of measuring as accurately as possible all phases of the higher mental functions cannot be overestimated. Stoddard ['25, p. 484] says, "The superior performance of superior students will be measured in part in ability to grasp more content, but it will be related content, different content, rather than more of the same thing. It is important to know the intricacies of his mental-educational relationships, what area he can cover; it is even more important to know the depth of these relationships, how high he can go. It is this hierarchical feature of learning that learning experiments carried out in linear fashion with simple material completely miss." Thorndike ['26] has pointed out the necessity and the technique of measuring the "altitude" of intelligence. He has produced many tasks with known degrees of difficulty in ". . . four lines of ability:

"C. To supply words so as to make a statement true and sensible.

"A. To solve arithmetical problems.

"V. To understand single words.

"D. To understand connected discourse as in oral direction or paragraph reading."

The completion sentence and the arithmetic problems, which are to be analyzed in the study, are included. These are tasks of the type of higher mental functions demanded by Stoddard.

The importance of an absolute zero cannot be emphasized too strongly in considering the accuracy of statistical descriptions. As has been previously mentioned, Thorndike ['04] called attention to the need of a known zero for measuring mental functions. Chapman ['25] showed the distortion of certain data by the lack of a known zero. He says [p. 226], "If we fail to interpret our figures in the light of the arbitrariness of the zero, we land ourselves in an absurd position when we use the ratio method of Reed. Thus employing an arbitrary scale with an arbitrary zero, the individual who improves from the arbitrary zero to the first point of the scale in a small period of practice has by the ratio method improved infinitely. This is the *reductio ad absurdum* of the procedure." Chapman [p. 226] gives the following diagram:

0 1 2 3 4 5 6 7 8 9 10   True Scale
         0 1 2 3 4 5   Arbitrary Scale

On a true scale, the distance from 0 to 2 is half that from 0 to 4, exactly as 4 inches is twice 2 inches. If, on our arbitrary scale, the origin is placed at 5 on the true scale, then on this arbitrary scale 4 is not twice 2, but merely 2 more than 2, for 2 on the arbitrary scale is in reality 7, and 4 on the arbitrary scale is in reality 9, and 9 is only 2 more than 7. This is a much smaller difference in reality on the true scale than it appears on the arbitrary scale and therefore any interpretation on the basis of the arbitrary scale will be distorted. The size of the error will be in proportion to the distance between the arbitrary zero and the true zero, the longer this distance the greater the error. Such tests as the Thorndike-McCall Reading

Scales, the National Intelligence Tests, and, in fact, all our educational and mental measurements, with the exception of the Thorndike CAVD Intelligence Tests and perhaps a few others, have only arbitrary zeros.   Therefore, any procedure in which a ratio of two scores is employed, where zero is arbitrary and not true, distorts the resulting data.   On scales of quality, especially handwriting, drawing, and sewing, a number of authors have attempted to get an approximately zero quality.   This is a great improvement, even though their approximate zero may be a long distance from true zero.   Thorndike ['26, p. 339] in discussing the absolute zero of intellectual difficulty states, "Just as we cannot properly add or subtract or average numbers representing degrees of intellectual difficulty until we know that the units called equal are really equal, so we cannot properly make the 'times as much' judgment, or divide one amount of intellectual difficulty by another to form a ratio, until we can state these amounts as differences from a true absolute zero meaning just barely not any intellectual difficulty."

An examination of the initial score in the learning tasks used in the above-mentioned experiments by Kincaid and others shows the zero points to be arbitrary.   If this error in experiments of this type can be corrected, we shall have scores that lend themselves to ratios and other derived units which are correct.

The tasks which go to make up the CAVD Intelligence Test of Thorndike have a known zero.[1]   As has been pointed out, they are tasks in the higher, more abstract, mental functions. Every requirement for the present study is found in these tasks.

Specifically, it is the purpose of this study to submit these

[1] It is not the province of this study to enter into either the validity or the reliability of the determination of the zero point.   The meaning of the values of these mental tasks is discussed in *The Measurement of Intelligence*.   To secure mental tasks of less reliability would be a marked step of improvement in an experiment of the nature herein described. It is sufficient to know that here is a set of tasks with an approximate absolute zero and a difficulty value based upon this zero point.   It is the use of tasks having these characteristics that is essential for this study and not the absolute exactness of the difficulty value of the tasks themselves.

C and A tasks to subjects under a plan similar to the practice exercises in learning experiments mentioned previously, and analyze the scores in the C and A tasks by the same methods employed in these learning experiments. It is believed that the findings will add to our knowledge of these higher mental functions as reliable measures of intelligence.

CHAPTER II

A DESCRIPTION OF THE C AND A TASKS AND THE EXPERIMENT

THE C AND A TASKS

THE C and A tasks used in this experiment are those described and illustrated by Thorndike ['26, pp. 66-94] in *The Measurement of Intelligence*. He and his associates had published in experimental form these CAVD tasks. The C and A tasks were printed (on paper eight and one-half by eleven inches) in order of difficulty, and space was provided for each response.[1] This form was used rather than the form which appeared subsequently in the CAVD Intelligence Tests. For the present study the completion tasks from 1 to 190[2] were bound in one booklet which will hereafter be referred to as booklet "C," and the arithmetic tasks from 1 to 210 were bound in another booklet which will hereafter be referred to as booklet "A." The printed directions to subjects at the top of each of the first pages were covered with paper, and oral directions (described later) were substituted.

SUBJECTS

The subjects of this experiment were pupils in grades 5, 6, and 7 in one ward school in Norman, Oklahoma. Their chronological ages ranged from 9 years and 5 months to 14 years and 10 months. Their mental ages (Detroit Intelligence Tests,

[1] These C and A tasks in this form were secured through the courtesy of Dr. Edward L. Thorndike, Division of Psychology, Institute of Educational Research, Teachers College, Columbia University.

[2] These identification numbers of all C and A tasks are the same as those appearing in the mimeographed bulletin, *The I.E.R. Inventory of Intellectual Tasks and Their Difficulty*, Bureau of Publications, Teachers College, Columbia University, 1926. The bulletin gives the values of all tasks from absolute zero.

Alpha Test, Form M) ranged from 8 years and 4 months to 14 years and 3 months. The data from this intelligence test were used only to select a group of about 100 children having a range of mental ages of approximately 6 years within one school building. This range seemed well adapted to the difficulties of the C and A tasks and presented a sufficient variability in intelligence to give a degree of accuracy necessary to interpret the data obtained from the experiment. The number of children follows: Grade 5, 40; Grade 6, 35; Grade 7, 31; a total of 106. From attendance reports it was estimated that with the experiment running approximately twenty days and with four additional days used to give intelligence tests, there would be approximately 90 to 100 cases with sufficient and complete data.

These pupils are relatively homogeneous in home environment and racial origin. They live in a section of the city with no distinctly poor element and no distinctly rich element. With the exception of a few Indians (in no case has any child more than one-eighth Indian blood) they are all Americans, speaking English from infancy. The occupations of the parents of these children are all within the so-called middle range from retired farmers to general retail merchants in a city of approximately 10,000 population. One parent is a college professor.

The teaching staff of these three grades has not changed within the last four years; neither has the supervisory staff, including the supervisor of grades, the principal of the building, and the superintendent of schools. There has been no distinctive change in the general educational policies within the past four years. This is about as homogeneous a group from the standpoint of general environmental conditions as could be found in any three grades.

THE EXPERIMENT

The general plan of the experiment follows closely after the practice exercise procedure of the learning experiments mentioned in Chapter I. Each day the "C" and "A" booklets were passed out to the children. Within each booklet, at the pages where children would be working for that day, were inserted mimeographed slips of paper called Response Sheets on which the children were instructed to write their responses. They were cautioned to write only on the Response Sheets. The position of writing on the Response Sheets is exactly the same as on the printed booklets. This permitted daily use of a new Response Sheet which would not show any previous responses, but would show the items on which a subject should work for the particular day. Response Sheets were scored and filed daily. Each subject was allowed four attempts to solve each C or A item. As soon as an item was solved the number of the item on a new Response Sheet for use the following day was crossed out with a heavy red pencil. Subjects were daily informed to work only the items whose numbers were not marked out, without being told why. Five minutes of clear working time was allowed for each booklet on each practice day. The order of working on the two booklets was changed daily to equalize any carry-over effect from one function to another. Since there were three grades in three different rooms and one examiner, a cycle was established to equalize the working periods among the three groups. The following schedule was used: on the first day the order of grades was 5, 6, and 7; on the second day the order of grades was 6, 7, and 5; on the third day the order was 7, 5, and 6. This cycle was repeated until the conclusion of the experiment. The work started each morning at nine o'clock, the first period in the school day.

In addition to the controls already described, a number of others were obtained and observed. All subjects had had previous experience in objective types of tests of the same form as those in the C and A tasks. During the experiment no problem in arithmetical reasoning or any type of problem that approached the type of reasoning involved in the arithmetic booklet was given in the arithmetic lesson or presented in any form. No completion sentence exercises or tests involving completion sentences were used in any subject outside of the experiment.

The teachers did not discuss any questions relative to the materials. Pupils were requested not to discuss any item with each other or with any one else. They were informed that they were helping the superintendent and the writer to find out facts about how boys and girls learn such things as are in these booklets. Parents made no objections to the experiment. Teachers were requested to listen to the comments of children for any indications of attitude. A number of comments indicated that the children were enjoying this intensive practice. Teachers and supervisors unanimously reported no evidence of outside work. Tardiness decreased during the experiment.

As soon as the subjects completed their work each day, the booklets were taken to a central office where the Response Sheets were removed from the booklets, numbered in agreement with the day of practice, scored, and filed under each subject's name, and new Response Sheets were inserted at the proper pages of each booklet. The scoring was done in part by, and under the direction of. the writer and three skilled clerical workers who were graduate students in educational measurements. These supervised the work of fifteen additional clerical workers who were undergraduate students in educational measurements. The accuracy of each worker was rechecked through a sampling technique by the three supervisors to determine those whose accuracy was almost perfect. Three workers were eliminated by this process, leaving twelve scorers who specialized on scoring Response Sheets and placing new Response Sheets in the different booklets.

While not all of the responses to the completion tasks were wholly objective, any special interpretation or shade of meaning varying from the key of answers was made by the writer and added to the key. The higher completion items were scored by the writer and the three supervisory students.

THE INTELLIGENCE TESTS

The following intelligence tests were administered at the beginning of the experiment: Otis Self-Administering Tests of

Mental Ability, Intermediate Examination, Forms A and B; McCall Multi-Mental Scale, Elementary School, Form 1; National Intelligence Tests, Scales A and B, Forms 1 and 2. The A and 1 forms were given first, immediately followed by the B and 2 forms. One test was given in the morning and one test was given in the afternoon. Since the McCall Multi-Mental Scale has only one form, it was the first and last test given. The data from the first tests only were used as measures of intelligence of the children. The data from the two forms were used to calculate reliabilities of the tests. All scoring was done under the same conditions and by the same clerical workers as for the C and A tasks.

CHAPTER III

THE DATA SECURED FROM THE EXPERIMENT AND THE MEASURES USED

THE PRIMARY DATA

THE Response Sheets containing all the responses, with the difficulty value of each correct response indicated and the intelligence tests scores, furnish the primary data which represent the measures of C and A tasks described under the specific conditions of the experiment. Instead of each correct response being counted one point, as is usually done, each correct response was converted into a difficulty value which was taken from The I.E.R. Inventory of Intellectual Tasks and Their Difficulty. The complete primary data then included the following: the identification number and difficulty value of each response for the C and A tasks attempted and correct each day, the scores on the four intelligence tests, the sum of the National Intelligence Tests Scales A and B, a combined intelligence test score based on all four of these tests, and the chronological ages of the children, as of the first day of the experiment. All of these data were entered on a large card for each child, but would require many pages if they were printed. Since this experiment is to evaluate certain scores in C and A similar to scores obtained in learning experiments, the essential data will be sought and only these are presented in this report.

THE UNITS OF MEASURE FOR TASKS C AND A

Before the essential data were recorded, an examination of the learning experiments mentioned in Chapter I was made to determine which scores are commonly used. These were found to be initial scores, final scores, gains, and per cent gains. These scores must be defined. The initial score will be defined as the average difficulty value of the first two days' practice score. In determining the definition of this score certain factors were considered. The subjects were already familiar with the objective types or forms in which the tasks were presented; they had already been working for several days on intelligence tests and had established the habit or attitude of responding to objective items, questions, and problems. They had taken a number of standardized achievement tests in their regular school work. The intelligence tests preceding the C and A tasks acted as a "warming up" or introductory practice exercise to the C and A tasks. The only distinctive difference between the two was the simple mechanics of writing C and A responses on inserted mimeographed slips of paper instead of writing responses in the booklets themselves. If there was any novelty the first day which would interfere with normal response, the interference was very small and was certainly completely overcome at the end of a first day's practice.

The final score will be defined as the average difficulty value of the last two days' practice score in which any item attempted was correct. The decision to take two days' score as the final score was based upon two facts: first, the final day was unknown to the children; second, many children made no scores on that day or, in a few cases, on several preceding days, because they had already reached their maximum altitude of difficulty. The reliability of a final score is conditioned by the number of tasks solved.

Gross gain score is defined as the difference between an initial and a final score. A factor affecting reliability of gross gain scores over a period of nineteen days is the number of practice periods between the initial and final score. The greater the number of these periods, the wider the differences in initial and final scores and, therefore, the more reliable the difference. The greater the number of days used to secure an initial score and the greater the number of days used to secure a final score the higher the reliability of the initial and final scores, but the fewer the number of days between the initial score and final score, and, therefore, the lower the reliability of gross gain scores. Increasing the reliability of one decreases the reliability of the other.

The reliability for the number of tasks solved in two days is much greater than the reliability for the number of tasks solved in one day. For two days n in the Brown-Spearman prophecy formula is almost double that for one day. But when the reliability of a gain score with initial and final scores based on the number of tasks solved in one day is compared with a gain score where the number of days for initial and final scores is doubled, the difference in reliability of the two gain scores is not large. The number of practice days between initial scores and final scores based on one day's practice is 17. The number of practice days between initial scores and final scores based on two days' practice is 15. In the second case, sampling of tasks worked is slightly less reliable than sampling of tasks worked in the first case. Therefore, doubling the number of days for counting responses for initial and final scores greatly raises the reliability of these scores and only slightly reduces the reliability of the gain score.

It was therefore decided to define gross gain as the gain between the arithmetic mean of the scores of the first two days and arithmetic mean of the scores of the last two days in which correct responses were made. Per cent gain will be the gross gain divided by the initial score.

Essential Primary Data

The primary data above can, then, be reduced in bulk to what will be called "essential primary data" for completely interpreting the facts that contribute to the problems of this experiment. Tables I and II present these essential primary data for the 97 cases whose records were included for the whole experiment. The data consist of: mean initial score (for first two days), mean final score (for last two days), mean gain (difference between mean initial and mean final scores), mean per

TABLE I

INITIAL SCORE, FINAL SCORE, GROSS GAIN, AND PER CENT GAIN IN
COMPLETION SENTENCES AND ARITHMETICAL PROBLEMS

Case No.	COMPLETION SENTENCES				ARITHMETICAL PROBLEMS			
	Initial Score	Final Score	Gross Gain	Per Cent Gain	Initial Score	Final Score	Gross Gain	Per Cent Gain
1	310	383	73	23.5	325	372	47	14.4
2	311	399	88	28.3	325	387	62	19.0
3	306	353	47	15.3	319	338	19	5.9
4	308	350	42	13.6	326	386	60	18.4
5	310	385	75	24.1	324	360	36	11.1
6	307	392	85	27.6	321	367	46	14.3
7	310	371	61	16.6	321	358	37	11.5
8	309	386	77	24.0	320	362	42	13.1
9	312	402	90	28.8	323	363	40	12.3
10	308	374	66	21.4	324	351	27	8.3
11	313	379	66	21.0	328	366	38	11.5
12	313	354	41	13.0	337	375	38	11.2
13	309	378	69	22.3	312	344	32	10.2
14	311	386	75	24.1	325	374	49	15.0
15	318	409	91	28.6	330	392	62	18.7
16	308	382	74	24.0	320	361	41	12.8
17	313	402	89	28.4	320	375	55	17.1
18	311	373	62	19.9	323	362	39	12.0
19	307	345	38	12.3	315	351	36	11.4
20	314	392	78	24.8	325	385	60	18.4
21	317	393	76	24.0	329	388	59	18.0
22	312	359	47	15.0	324	367	43	13.2
23	318	404	86	22.0	326	381	55	16.8
24	310	381	71	22.9	318	344	26	8.1
25	310	368	58	18.7	320	358	38	11.8
26	307	358	51	16.6	319	335	16	5.0
27	311	400	89	28.6	320	355	35	10.9
28	310	375	65	20.9	320	368	48	15.0
29	311	397	86	27.6	321	380	59	18.3
30	315	380	65	20.6	326	356	30	9.2
31	316	393	77	24.3	319	354	35	10.9
32	315	399	84	26.6	317	365	48	15.1
33	311	370	59	18.9	321	350	29	9.0
34	306	367	61	19.9	322	353	31	9.6
35	307	392	85	27.6	322	375	53	16.4
36	309	381	72	23.3	320	361	41	12.8
37	318	401	83	26.1	321	355	34	10.5
38	310	381	71	22.9	327	371	44	13.4
39	313	402	89	28.4	323	358	35	10.8
40	318	374	56	17.6	326	370	44	13.4
41	307	341	34	11.0	322	349	27	8.3
42	309	378	69	21.3	324	353	29	8.9
43	313	388	75	23.9	331	367	36	10.8
44	309	370	61	11.7	316	376	60	18.9

TABLE I (*Continued*)

Case No.	COMPLETION SENTENCES				ARITHMETICAL PROBLEMS			
	Initial Score	Final Score	Gross Gain	Per Cent Gain	Initial Score	Final Score	Gross Gain	Per Cent Gain
45	307	363	56	18.2	324	360	36	11.1
46	312	368	56	17.9	322	357	35	10.8
47	310	400	90	29.0	329	362	33	10.0
48	308	371	63	20.4	325	360	35	10.7
49	311	362	51	16.3	323	353	30	9.2
50	318	402	84	26.4	323	371	49	15.1
51	310	359	47	15.8	325	354	30	8.9
52	306	342	36	12.0	318	346	28	9.0
53	308	354	46	14.9	323	350	27	8.3
54	316	396	80	25.3	325	379	54	16.6
55	309	401	92	29.7	323	382	59	18.2
56	307	363	56	18.2	312	349	37	11.8
57	310	392	82	26.4	325	392	67	20.6
58	316	392	76	24.0	324	376	52	16.0
59	310	392	82	26.4	325	373	48	14.7
60	317	398	81	25.5	330	366	36	10.0
61	306	365	59	19.2	303	352	54	16.1
62	312	396	84	26.9	320	361	41	12.8
63	307	386	79	26.0	320	364	44	13.7
64	308	368	60	19.4	318	348	30	9.4
65	315	386	71	22.5	329	375	46	13.9
66	312	398	85	27.2	322	378	56	17.3
67	320	393	73	22.8	328	383	58	17.8
68	308	403	95	30.8	325	376	51	15.6
69	310	405	95	30.6	325	386	61	18.7
70	311	372	61	19.6	320	354	34	10.6
71	310	372	62	20.0	312	358	46	14.7
72	309	401	92	29.7	323	358	35	10.8
73	308	373	65	21.1	320	350	30	9.3
74	321	394	73	22.7	329	380	51	15.5
75	309	381	72	23.3	322	376	54	16.7
76	309	392	83	26.8	315	368	53	16.8
77	309	399	90	29.1	321	352	31	9.6
78	317	377	60	18.9	321	356	35	10.9
79	310	370	60	19.3	319	365	46	14.4
80	305	368	63	20.6	320	350	30	9.3
81	315	408	93	29.5	326	374	48	14.7
82	311	382	71	22.8	320	376	56	17.5
83	306	354	48	15.6	319	367	48	15.0
84	313	388	75	23.9	322	386	64	19.8
85	308	366	58	18.8	320	348	28	8.7
86	307	366	59	19.2	319	348	29	9.0
87	310	397	87	28.3	323	370	47	14.4
88	313	402	89	28.4	322	359	37	11.4
89	308	391	83	26.9	319	358	39	12.2
90	316	370	54	17.0	325	356	31	9.5

TABLE I (*Continued*)

Case No.	COMPLETION SENTENCES				ARITHMETICAL PROBLEMS			
	Initial Score	Final Score	Gross Gain	Per Cent Gain	Initial Score	Final Score	Gross Gain	Per Cent Gain
91	313	391	78	24.9	323	357	34	10.5
92	312	403	91	29.1	321	387	66	20.5
93	308	368	60	19.4	320	350	30	9.3
94	316	396	80	25.3	328	390	62	18.9
95	307	359	52	16.9	322	360	38	11.8
96	307	365	58	18.8	319	358	39	12.2
97	308	377	69	22.4	324	361	37	11.4

TABLE II

CHRONOLOGICAL AGE AND SCORES ON OTIS, McCALL MULTI-MENTAL, NATIONAL SCALE A, NATIONAL SCALE B, NATIONAL A AND B COMBINED, AND ALL TESTS COMBINED

Case No.	Age	Otis	McCall	TEST SCORE			All Tests
				National A	National B	National A and B	
1	150	59	66	116	130	246	58.79
2	152	58	60	153	135	288	62.94
3	147	19	40	65	80	145	19.70
4	150	58	56	125	141	266	57.36
5	153	55	60	137	90	227	51.91
6	133	47	54	128	131	259	52.48
7	134	60	65	151	142	293	66.56
8	127	47	48	138	133	271	51.78
9	113	41	50	107	107	214	41.53
10	127	36	43	105	99	204	35.39
11	159	46	55	129	126	255	52.01
12	151	28	53	86	105	191	35.67
13	127	29	46	103	118	221	37.81
14	134	57	48	130	145	275	54.98
15	154	66	67	159	163	322	73.87
16	148	37	56	105	141	246	48.60
17	144	47	50	128	122	250	49.15
18	168	46	61	130	118	248	53.57
19	139	15	39	113	92	205	28.41
20	128	53	59	136	145	281	59.99
21	141	66	67	140	151	291	68.63
22	154	42	43	123	120	243	43.50
23	157	47	62	144	160	304	70.58
24	145	36	49	108	108	216	40.14
25	137	35	48	102	109	211	38.58
26	161	30	48	109	117	226	39.83
27	146	35	54	105	120	225	43.66
28	117	40	30	138	112	250	47.39
29	155	45	62	121	137	258	55.42
30	136	45	58	112	130	242	50.90

TABLE II (*Continued*)

Case No.	Age	Otis	McCall	Test Score National A	National B	National A and B	All Tests
31	144	41	59	133	123	256	52.73
32	127	54	60	150	158	308	65.24
33	126	39	41	123	148	271	46.52
34	113	31	44	106	106	212	35.91
35	155	68	67	136	130	266	64.94
36	159	54	57	133	133	266	56.81
37	125	41	61	135	139	274	56.66
38	177	40	50	105	93	198	38.59
39	137	63	55	141	141	282	60.90
40	125	46	55	128	149	277	55.72
41	132	34	48	103	111	214	38.84
42	150	48	62	136	134	270	58.24
43	125	43	50	99	110	209	41.18
44	140	43	61	142	112	254	53.84
45	134	33	42	96	86	182	30.46
46	143	24	47	100	104	204	39.13
47	145	57	57	119	131	250	57.11
48	134	49	49	123	147	270	52.54
49	176	41	47	117	118	235	43.71
50	135	51	60	117	136	253	55.19
51	131	45	49	118	148	266	50.84
52	161	15	37	58	83	141	16.64
53	149	34	48	99	118	217	39.32
54	125	62	61	151	140	291	64.91
55	148	64	64	133	148	281	65.06
56	135	34	51	107	116	223	41.71
57	136	66	53	141	143	284	61.09
58	163	47	51	121	126	247	49.08
59	168	62	62	141	140	281	63.66
60	126	41	45	117	119	236	42.97
61	126	28	44	82	88	170	28.05
62	145	52	50	118	112	230	47.05
63	129	48	55	125	123	248	51.09
64	144	47	47	113	130	243	46.57
65	148	53	52	112	144	256	52.55
66	147	48	53	125	120	245	49.92
67	142	66	70	157	162	319	74.73
68	142	43	53	121	134	255	50.31
69	137	61	59	139	138	277	62.87
70	176	31	44	100	114	214	36.23
71	134	43	47	102	121	223	42.17
72	167	44	63	125	152	277	58.81
73	140	44	49	120	134	254	48.58
74	186	55	60	151	138	289	62.34
75	131	52	56	116	128	244	52.12
76	162	49	55	114	130	244	50.64
77	126	23	43	100	99	199	31.23

TABLE II (*Continued*)

Case No.	Age	Otis	McCall	Test Score National A	National B	National A and B	All Tests
78	138	52	61	120	138	258	56.75
79	122	57	51	122	105	227	52.88
80	143	45	56	120	126	246	50.80
81	137	69	66	156	153	309	72.00
82	159	51	63	141	131	272	59.81
83	128	35	45	90	117	207	36.51
84	161	53	62	138	159	297	64.04
85	138	43	48	114	141	255	48.02
86	124	29	43	77	97	174	28.50
87	149	45	53	135	125	260	51.70
88	137	50	58	153	143	296	61.33
89	164	24	47	77	114	191	31.90
90	113	37	50	131	122	253	47.11
91	128	55	56	136	139	275	58.13
92	138	67	59	164	145	309	68.33
93	129	40	47	111	129	240	44.28
94	147	51	66	142	154	296	65.14
95	131	45	41	104	108	212	38.11
96	135	31	43	99	99	198	33.09
97	133	31	50	95	108	203	37.11

cent gain (mean gain divided by mean initial score) for tasks C and A; the scores on all of the intelligence tests, the combined score[1] on all intelligence tests; and chronological age.

THE MEASURES USED

The statistical measures used to interpret the data for tasks C and A are those found common to most of the learning experiments previously mentioned. These measures, thirteen in all, follow: (1) a comparison of absolute differences at beginning and end of practice periods by use of the standard deviations; (2) a comparison of relative differences at beginning and end of practice periods by use of the coefficient of variability; (3) a comparison of the initial ratio between worse and better scores with final ratio between worse and better scores; (4) a comparison of the absolute gross gain of the upper quartile

[1] Scores combined as described by Clark Hull, "The Conversion of Test Scores into Series Which Shall Have Any Assigned Mean and Degree of Dispersion," *Journal of Applied Psychology,* 1922, p. 299.

group in initial scores with the absolute gross gain of the lower quartile group in initial scores; (5) a comparison of the relative gain (per cent gain) of the upper quartile group in initial scores with the relative gain of the lower quartile group in initial scores; (6) a comparison of gross gains of the upper quartile group in intelligence test scores with the gross gains of the lower quartile group in intelligence test scores; (7) a comparison of the relative gains of the upper quartile group in intelligence test scores with the relative gains of the lower quartile group in intelligence test scores; (8) correlation between initial scores and gross gains; (9) correlation between initial scores and per cent gains; (10) correlation between intelligence scores and initial scores; (11) correlation between intelligence scores and final scores; (12) correlation between intelligence scores and gross gains; and (13) correlation between intelligence scores and relative gains.

The units of measure used in this study and described above are arbitrary to a large extent. The purpose we have in mind determines the units of measurements. The importance of the interpretations of the data from this study, therefore, hinges on the units herein defined. This fact has been pointed out by Kelley[2] and should always be taken into consideration in interpreting such data. It is further understood that any interpretation of these measures must always be made in terms of the reliability of the original units themselves, and the limits of accurate interpretation are set up by these errors. Some of these are not within the control of the experimenter and are not easily arrived at statistically. The gain scores secured in this experiment are based on absolute zeros. Per cent gains are true ratios and do not have the errors pointed out by Chapman ['25] and explained above. Since gross gains are measured from absolute zeros, per cent gains are not necessary for a complete interpretation of the data presented here, but they will be given to afford possible comparisons with other studies.

[2] National Research Council, *Conference on Individual Psychological Differences*, p. 12. Washington, D. C., 1930.

CHAPTER IV

STATISTICAL INTERPRETATION OF THE MEASURES OBTAINED IN THE EXPERIMENT

Measures of Variability of Initial and Final Scores

The general status in the C and A tasks of the 97 children whose work was sufficiently complete to use is shown in Table III by the mean initial score, mean final score, their differences, the significance of their differences, mean gross gain, mean per cent gain, and the standard errors of these units. It is obvious that the final scores in all cases will be larger than the initial scores because the tasks were arranged in order of difficulty. The gross gain is a true linear measure of gain or altitude under the conditions of the experiment because the units of the scale are equal and are based on an absolute zero. The gross gain in completion sentences is 70.37 ± 1.52 and the gross gain in arithmetical problems is 42.16 ± 1.17. The standard deviations of these gains are relatively large: 15.06 ± 1.08 for the former and $11.53 \pm .82$ for the latter. The per cent gain in completion sentences is $22.63 \pm .50$ and the per cent gain in arithmetical problems is $13.08 \pm .36$. These represent true ratio gains because the numerators and denominators are measured from absolute zeros. It is, of course, obvious that the mean difference between initial and final scores will be statistically significant.

The maximum altitude scores attained by these students in tasks C and A are not the same; neither are the gross gain scores the same.

The gain in tasks A is less than the gain in tasks C. The exact cause for this cannot be determined from the data available. However, in tasks C the average difficulty for the first

30 tasks is 307.2 and in tasks A the average difficulty for the first 30 tasks is 319.9. If we consider any particular section higher up the scale as tasks numbered 141-150, the average difficulty for tasks C is 419.3, making a total possible gain for the mean of the first 30 tasks of 112.1 points, and the average difficulty for a similar section in tasks A is 384.6, making a possible gain of 65 points. This gives a

TABLE III

MEAN INITIAL SCORE, MEAN FINAL SCORE, MEAN GAIN, MEAN PER CENT GAIN, AND STATISTICAL DIFFERENCE BETWEEN INITIAL AND FINAL SCORES ON COMPLETION SENTENCES AND ARITHMETICAL PROBLEMS

Record	For Completion Sentences	For Arithmetical Problems
Mean Initial Score	310.91 ± .37*	322.20 ± .45
Mean Final Score	381.28 ± 1.69	364.36 ± 1.32
Mean Gain	70.37 ± 1.52	42.16 ± 1.17
Standard Error of Gain†	1.52	1.17
Gain/Standard Error of Gain	45.99	36.03
Mean Per Cent Gain	22.63 ± .50	13.08 ± .36

* Standard error.

† The formula used is $\sigma_{dif} = \sqrt{\sigma_I^2 + \sigma_F^2 - 2r_{IF}\sigma_I\sigma_F}$ (I represents initial score and F represents final score).

greater opportunity to gain in tasks C than in tasks A. It is recognized that the type of mental function performed in tasks A is practiced very little by children of this age outside of school. They performed no arithmetical operations in school (as far as could be controlled by teachers and supervisors) and they probably practiced very little arithmetic outside of school. They did have practice of a certain kind in tasks similar to tasks C, as these are linguistic. Children were speaking, writing, and hearing words and sentences all during the experiment. As a matter of fact, a great many questions that teachers ask in school, in practically all subjects, are in a measure similar to completion exercises. Consequently, there were some factors in the organization of the experiment that can be controlled and some factors that cannot be controlled. These uncontrolled factors may account for different altitudes in tasks C and A. It is a difficult matter to get at the factors within the individual that make his "internal" environments distinct, for these factors are so heavily influenced by difference in nurture prior to the experiment that they cannot be measured or held constant by an experimental situation. In other words, previous conditioning might be as potent as present environment, and could, in itself, account for differences at the end of the practice periods.

Absolute difference is best expressed by a comparison of the standard deviations of the initial and final scores. The larger the standard deviations at the end of the practice period the wider the difference. In Table IV are presented these standard deviations with their standard errors. The standard deviation in tasks C for initial scores is only 3.66 ± .26 and for final scores the standard deviation is 16.64 ± 1.19. The standard deviations in tasks A for initial scores is only 4.51 ± .32 and for final scores the standard deviation is 13.03 ± .93.

Relative variabilities in terms of the means of the initial scores and the means of the final scores are expressed by the coefficients of variability. They are calculated by the formula

$$V = \frac{100 \times \sigma}{M}$$

and its standard error[1]

$$\sigma_V = \frac{V}{\sqrt{2N}}$$

These coefficients and their standard errors for the initial scores, final scores, gross gains, and per cent gains are given in Table V. The important comparisons are the coefficients of variability of the initial and of the final scores. For both tasks C and A the final coefficients of variability are much larger than the initial coefficients. The coefficients of variability of

[1] Yule, G. Udny, *An Introduction to the Theory of Statistics,* Charles Griffin and Company, Ltd., 1924, pp. 351 and 352, gives the following formula and comment: "The standard error of coefficient of $\sigma_V = \frac{V}{\sqrt{2n}}\left\{ 1 + 2\left(\frac{V}{100}\right)^2 \right\}^{\frac{1}{2}}$ The expression in the brackets is usually very nearly unity, for a normal distribution, and in that case may be neglected." This formula was used without the term in the bracket.

gains and per cent gains are shown for comparisons between the tasks C and A. Both absolute and relative measures of variability show greater variability at the end of the experimental periods than at the beginning of the experimental periods. Since all known factors that could affect responses were held constant during the nineteen days in which subjects worked on these tasks, we have only differences due to native ability

TABLE IV

STANDARD DEVIATIONS OF INITIAL SCORES, FINAL SCORES, GAINS, AND
PER CENT GAINS IN COMPLETION SENTENCES AND ARITHMETICAL
PROBLEMS

Record	STANDARD DEVIATION	
	For Completion Sentences	For Arithmetical Problems
Initial Score	3.66 ± .26*	4.51 ± .32
Final Score	16.64 ± 1.19	13.03 ± .93
Gain	15.06 ± 1.08	11.53 ± .82
Per Cent Gain	4.92 ± .35	3.52 ± .25

* Standard error.

or intelligence to explain the increase in variability. Evidently the altitudes of intelligence varied greatly amongst these subjects, as the tasks were arranged in order of difficulty; the majority of students on the nineteenth day evidently were working on tasks beyond their altitude, since they made no correct responses for the last day.

TABLE V

COEFFICIENTS OF VARIABILITY FOR INITIAL SCORES, FINAL SCORES, GAINS,
AND PER CENT GAINS IN COMPLETION SENTENCES AND
ARITHMETICAL PROBLEMS

Record	COEFFICIENT OF VARIABILITY	
	For Completion Sentences	For Arithmetical Problems
Initial Scores	1.17 ± .08*	1.39 ± .10
Final Scores	4.36 ± .31	3.57 ± .25
Gains	21.32 ± 1.53	27.26 ± 1.95
Per Cent Gains	22.30 ± 1.60	24.14 ± 1.73

* Standard error.

Another measure of variability as used by Kincaid ['25, p. 44] and others, and expressed by the ratio of the worse and better records, indicates an increase in variability from initial to final scores.   While these units of variability lack adequate sampling (one extreme and one next-to-extreme case in each term), they indicate a tendency which, if the same in all other data, assists in substantiating the significance of these differences.   These data are presented in Table VI.   The score in each term is given, as these ratios do not have a constant de-

TABLE VI

RATIOS OF INITIAL WORST AND INITIAL BEST SCORE (IW/IB), FINAL WORST
AND FINAL BEST SCORE (FW/FB), INITIAL NEXT WORST AND INITIAL
NEXT BEST SCORE (INW/INB) AND FINAL NEXT WORST AND FINAL
NEXT BEST SCORE (FNW/FNB) IN C AND A TASKS

Record	RATIO	
	For Completion Sentences	For Arithmetical Problems
IW/IB	305/321 = .950	303/337 = .899
FW/FB	341/409 = .833	335/392 = .854
Gain (F − I)	.117	.045
INW/INB	306/320 = .956	312/331 = .942
FNW/FNB	342/408 = .838	338/390 = .866
Gain (F − I)	.118	.076

nominator and are difficult to interpret without both numerator and denominator.   These ratios substantiate the findings shown by the absolute and relative measures of variability.

COMPARISONS OF SCORES OF INITIALLY HIGH AND LOW GROUPS

Another set of measures that will yield data relative to the effect of intelligence on the functions C and A will be the final scores, gross gains, and per cent gains of a low group and of a high group selected by initial scores.   For this purpose the lowest 25 per cent, on the basis of initial scores, are chosen as the low group (designated in the tables by the symbol Lq, lower than first quartile); and the highest 25 per cent, on the basis of initial scores, are chosen as the high group (designated by the symbol Uq, higher than the third quartile).   A complete statistical description of all means, sigmas, and coefficients of variability of both groups is given in Table VII showing the following: mean initial scores and their sigmas (items 1-4); mean final scores and their sigmas (items 5-8); the differences of the final scores and their significances (items 9-11); the mean gross gains, their sigmas, differences, and significances (items 12-18); the mean per cent gains, their sigmas, differ-

TABLE VII

COMPARISON OF LOWER AND UPPER QUARTER GROUPS (Lq AND Uq) WITH RESPECT TO MEAN INITIAL SCORES (M I), MEAN FINAL SCORES (M F), MEAN GAINS (M G), MEAN PER CENT GAINS (M %), AND COEFFICIENTS OF VARIABILITY, ON COMPLETION SENTENCES AND ARITHMETICAL PROBLEMS

Record	For Completion Sentences	For Arithmetical Problems
1. M ILq	307.23 ± 1.12*	317.10 ± 1.42
2. σ ILq	$5.49 \pm .79$	6.98 ± 1.00
3. M IUq	316.21 ± 1.34	327.53 ± 1.40
4. σ IUq	$6.73 \pm .97$	7.01 ± 1.01
5. M FLq	363.91 ± 2.78	353.16 ± 1.93
6. σ FLq	$13.62 \pm .19$	9.59 ± 1.38
7. M FUq	393.91 ± 2.10	377.25 ± 2.04
8. σ FUq	10.29 ± 1.48	10.25 ± 1.44
9. Dif (FUq − FLq)	30.00	24.09
10. σ dif/†	3.33	2.81
11. Dif/σ dif	8.98	8.56
12. M GLq	56.68 ± 2.71	36.06 ± 2.21
13. σ GLq	13.30 ± 1.91	10.84 ± 1.56
14. M GUq	77.70 ± 2.12	49.72 ± 2.29
15. σ GUq	10.39 ± 1.50	11.24 ± 1.62
16. Dif (GUq − GLq)	21.02	13.66
17. σ dif	3.44	3.18
18. Dif/σ dif	6.10	4.38
19. M %GLq	$18.49 \pm .88$	$11.38 \pm .94$
20. σ %GLq	$4.34 \pm .62$	$4.62 \pm .66$
21. M %GUq	$24.35 \pm .69$	$15.08 \pm .70$
22. σ %GUq	$3.39 \pm .49$	$3.46 \pm .49$
23. Dif (%GUq − %GLq)	5.86	3.70
24. σ dif	1.12	1.18
25. Dif/σ dif	5.20	3.13
26. V ILq	$1.78 \pm .12$	$2.20 \pm .15$
27. V IUq	$2.12 \pm .15$	$2.14 \pm .15$
28. V FLq	$3.74 \pm .54$	$2.71 \pm .39$
29. V FUq	$2.61 \pm .37$	$2.66 \pm .38$
30. V GLq	23.46 ± 3.37	30.06 ± 4.06
31. V GUq	14.29 ± 1.93	22.60 ± 3.27
32. V %GLq	23.95 ± 3.40	40.56 ± 5.42
33. V %GUq	13.95 ± 2.01	22.93 ± 3.30

* Standard error.

† The formula used is: $\sigma_{dif} = \sqrt{\sigma_{FUq}^2 + \sigma_{FLq}^2}$

TABLE VIII

COMPARISON OF LOWER QUARTER AND UPPER QUARTER GROUPS (Lq AND Uq) WITH RESPECT TO MEAN INITIAL SCORE (M I), MEAN FINAL SCORE (M F), MEAN GAIN (M G), AND MEAN PER CENT GAIN (M %G) ON COMPLETION SENTENCES AND ARITHMETICAL PROBLEMS

(The quartile groups are based on intelligence test scores.)

Record	Otis C	Otis A	McCall C	McCall A	National A C	National A A	National B C	National B A	National AB C	National AB A	Combined C	Combined A
1. M IIq	308.16 ±.57*	319.62 ±1.24	308.58 ±.60	320.43 ±1.26	308.62 ±.56	320.62 ±.83	308.72 ±1.14	321.37 ±1.25	308.56 ±.46	321.28 ±1.38	308.12 ±.53	320.33 ±1.21
2. σ IIq	2.84	6.08	2.98	6.24	2.76	4.07	5.61	6.14	2.27	6.77	2.61	5.96
3. M IUq	312.75 ±.77	324.41 ±.77	312.91 ±1.39	323.70 ±1.06	313.08 ±.76	323.70 ±.86	312.95 ±.86	324.29 ±1.45	313.83 ±1.17	324.04 ±.67	313.16 ±.86	324.29 ±.65
4. σ IUq	3.78	3.78	6.84	5.20	3.75	4.24	4.23	7.15	5.74	3.32	4.25	3.21
5. Dif (IUq − IIq)	4.59	4.79	4.33	3.66	4.46	3.08	4.25	2.92	5.33	2.76	5.04	3.96
6. σ dif	.96	1.45	1.51	1.64	.95	1.27	1.42	1.91	6.17	7.49	1.01	1.38
7. Dif/σ dif	4.76	3.28	2.85	2.22	4.69	2.57	2.97	1.52	4.13	1.78	2.95	1.86
8. M FLq	366.58 ±3.18	352.70 ±1.79	366.62 ±3.00	353.16 ±1.67	369.41 ±3.47	356.25 ±1.30	369.08 ±3.18	358.70 ±2.09	365.62 ±2.94	355.95 ±1.82	367.87 ±3.35	353.83 ±1.92
9. σ FLq	15.60	8.81	14.72	8.21	17.03	6.40	15.59	10.24	14.41	8.90	16.43	9.39
10. M FUq	392.87 ±2.60	376.12 ±2.25	391.29 ±2.85	373.83 ±2.38	389.56 ±2.86	373.66 ±2.77	393.00 ±2.02	376.87 ±2.33	395.43 ±.73	376.84 ±.84	395.46 ±.70	375.65 ±2.68
11. σ FUq	12.76	11.06	14.00	11.70	14.04	13.57	9.90	11.42	3.60	4.12	3.46	13.15
12. Dif (FUq − IIq)	26.29	23.42	24.67	20.67	20.09	17.41	23.92	18.17	29.78	20.85	27.53	21.77

13. σ dif	4.11	2.88	4.14	2.91	4.50	3.06	3.77	3.13	3.02	2.00	3.47	3.29
14. Dif/σ dif	6.39	8.13	5.95	7.08	4.41	5.68	6.34	5.80	9.86	10.42	8.04	6.60
15. M GLq	58.41 ±3.03	33.29 ±1.63	58.04 ±2.73	34.00 ±1.69	60.79 ±3.01	35.63 ±1.57	59.08 ±3.00	36.25 ±1.50	59.36 ±3.13	34.86 ±1.54	57.12 ±3.69	33.70 ±1.70
16. σ GLq	14.85	8.01	13.40	8.30	14.77	7.72	14.73	7.38	15.35	7.56	18.05	8.36
17. M GUq	79.25 ±2.48	50.87 ±2.11	78.16 ±2.08	50.16 ±2.08	80.08 ±1.93	53.16 ±2.01	76.45 ±2.67	48.08 ±2.55	81.62 ±1.98	52.29 ±2.10	82.29 ±1.78	51.62 ±2.27
18. σ GUq	12.19	10.35	10.21	10.23	9.48	9.85	13.10	12.53	9.73	10.47	8.71	11.33
19. Dif (GUq − GLq)	20.84	17.58	20.12	16.16	19.29	17.53	17.37	11.83	22.26	17.43	25.09	17.91
20. σ dif	3.92	2.67	3.43	2.68	3.58	2.55	4.02	2.96	3.70	2.60	4.09	2.83
21. Dif/σ dif	5.31	6.58	5.85	6.01	5.38	6.86	4.31	3.98	5.96	6.70	6.12	6.32
22. M %GLq	18.91 ±.98	10.35 ±1.31	19.29 ±.83	10.86 ±.47	19.66 ±.96	11.05 ±.65	19.15 ±1.02	11.31 ±.57	19.20 ±1.00	10.75 ±.62	18.57 ±.92	10.45 ±.53
23. σ %GLq	4.81	6.35	4.08	2.32	4.72	3.18	4.99	2.79	4.89	3.06	4.52	2.64
24. M %GUq	24.99 ±.84	15.63 ±.64	23.97 ±.86	15.11 ±.46	24.72 ±.82	16.05 ±.47	24.08 ±.86	14.76 ±.79	25.65 ±.73	16.05 ±.66	25.87 ±.68	15.89 ±.70
25. σ %GUq	4.15	3.14	4.21	3.15	4.04	2.34	4.23	3.87	3.58	3.23	3.33	3.45
26. Dif (%GUq − %GLq)	6.08	5.28	4.68	4.25	5.06	5.00	4.93	3.45	6.45	5.30	7.30	5.49
27. σ dif	1.28	1.83	1.29	.65	1.27	.80	1.33	.97	1.23	.90	1.14	.87
28. Dif/σ dif	4.75	2.85	3.98	6.53	3.97	6.18	3.70	3.55	5.24	5.83	6.40	6.31

* The figures preceded by ± represent the standard errors of the mean scores presented directly above.

ences, and significances (items 19-25); and the coefficients of variability of the initial scores, final scores, gross gains, and per cent gains (items 26-33). These data indicate that the initially higher group obtain a higher final score, larger gross gain, and a larger per cent gain in both C and A tasks, and the difference in each case is statistically significant. In functions C and A the initially low students and the initially high students will probably always retain their positions at the end of an experiment when measured by final scores, gross gains, and per cent gains.

Comparisons of Initial Scores, Final Scores, Gains, and Per Cent Gains of Bright and of Dull Subjects

Another group of measures that will give the influence of intelligence on tasks C and A can be determined by dividing the subjects of this experiment into dull and bright groups on the basis of intelligence test scores and comparing their initial scores, final scores, gross gains, and per cent gains. The highest 25 per cent on intelligence test scores are chosen as the upper group. The lowest 25 per cent on intelligence test scores are chosen as the low group. Since the subjects were given intelligence tests Otis, McCall, National A, and National B, the comparison between the bright and the dull group will be made on the basis of each of these tests and on certain combinations of the tests. The National A and B scores were summated arithmetically. The scores on all the intelligence tests were combined as previously described. The combined scores are given in the last column in Table II.

For the upper and lower groups for each intelligence test, for National A and B combined, and for all intelligence tests combined, the following data are given in Table VIII: the mean initial scores for the upper and lower groups, their sigmas, differences, and significance of differences (items 1-7); the mean final scores for the upper and lower groups, their sigmas, differences, and significance of differences (items 8-14); the mean gain scores for the upper and lower groups, their sigmas, differences, and significance of differences (items 15-21); and the mean per cent score for the upper and lower groups, their sigmas, differences, and significance of differences (items 22-28).

The difference between the mean initial scores of the upper and lower groups is statistically significant for task A when the groups are chosen on the basis of Otis scores, but not significant under any other intelligence test or intelligence scores combined, although the difference is in favor of the upper group. The differences between the mean initial scores, mean final scores, mean gains, and mean per cent gains of the upper and lower groups are all significant under all intelligence tests and combined intelligence tests scores. The difference is always in favor of the upper group. We may conclude from these data in Table VIII that a group of bright subjects, chosen on the basis of several of the stock general intelligence tests, will attain higher altitude scores in both tasks C and A. The only factor we have measured which will account for this is intelligence. The intelligence that functions in tasks C and A under the conditions of this experiment is largely the same as that measured by the general intelligence tests used to select the bright and dull groups. This is the same conclusion reached by Thorndike ['26, p. 107] in reviewing the correlations of Clark ['24].

RELATIONSHIP BETWEEN INITIAL SCORE AND FINAL SCORE

Another method of analyzing the relationship between initial scores and final scores is by correlating initial measures with

TABLE IX

CORRELATIONS BETWEEN INITIAL SCORES AND FINAL SCORES, INITIAL SCORES AND GAINS, AND INITIAL SCORES AND PER CENT GAINS ON COMPLETION SENTENCES AND ARITHMETICAL PROBLEMS

Measures Correlated	COMPLETION SENTENCES		ARITHMETICAL PROBLEMS	
	r	P.E.	*r*	P.E.
Initial Scores and Final Scores	.526	± .0495	.493	± .0517
Initial Scores and Gains	.351	± .0607	.237	± .0651
Initial Scores and Per Cent Gains	.276	± .0635	.150	± .0671

final measures. These correlations are given in Table IX. Thorndike ['24] pointed out the inaccuracies in such correlations due to errors of initial and final scores, and Thomson ['24] submitted formula with proof to correct such errors. The advisability of the use of this formula depends upon the practicability of securing coefficients of reliability for initial and final scores, but it has been pointed out above that it is almost impossible to secure these reliabilities because of the ease of the first and second day's tasks and the small number of tasks correctly completed on the eighteenth and nineteenth days (or last and next to last days). This, regardless of its desirability, prevents the use of Thomson's formula. According to this formula, corrected correlations will be higher than the uncorrected correlations, because of spuriousness caused by correlating errors. Therefore, the probability is that the true relationships between initial scores and final scores will be higher than those presented in Table IX.

It will be noticed from Table IX that there is a slight difference in the correlation between initial and final scores in tasks C and A, .526 and .493 respectively. If these correlations could be corrected by Thomson's formula, it is very probable that the correlation for tasks C and A would be considerably increased. This means that if we have reliable initial and final scores we could accurately predict a final score from the initial score in tasks C and A. However, gains and per cent gains are not so closely related to initial scores. The correlations between initial scores and gains and between initial scores and per cent gains are significant but low when compared with their probable errors. Since the gains and per cent gains involve the initial scores, any correlation between initial scores and any other scores derived by a use of initial scores will be affected by the reliability of the initial scores. We therefore expect these correlations to be lower than the correlations between initial and final scores. If the reliabilities of initial scores are lower than those of final scores, this will make the correlations between initial scores and gains or per cent gains still lower. It appears that lack of perfect reliability has affected these'correlations in this manner.

Hunsiker ['25] correlated a *rate* and *level* score for tasks C and A. The rate score is the reciprocal of total time on the first two sheets of the I.E.R. Arithmetical Problems and the first two sheets of the I.E.R. Completions. The level score was based on a score on two sheets of tasks C and A of greater difficulty. Her correlations [p. 32] between rate and level for arithmetic range from .29 $\pm$ .12 to .49 $\pm$ .09 and for completion from .19 $\pm$ .09 to .50 $\pm$ .10. There is undoubtedly the influence of rate on initial scores of the present experiment and certainly the influence of level (as pointed out above) in final scores. The differences in the correlations in the two studies are not great, but her unit of measure for rate is very different from the unit of measure for initial score in the present experiment, and this makes any comparison between the two sets of correlations difficult to interpret.

RELATIONSHIP BETWEEN SCORES IN TASKS C AND A AND INTELLIGENCE

Another measure of the effect of intelligence, as measured by stock intelligence tests, on scores in tasks C and A is the correlations between these two sets of variables.

The size of any correlation in which C and A scores are variables will depend, of course, upon their own reliability. Two factors which may not work together (as previously pointed out in determining the measures of initial score, final score, and gains) in yielding a high reliability must be considered: first, the reliability of the initial and final scores, which have already been discussed, and, second, the reliability of the gain. The reliability of gain score can be determined by the correlation between two measures of gain with the number of practice periods between the initial and final scores the same for both sets of gain scores. It is obvious that the distance from the first day to the eighteenth day (or next to the last day on which there was any correct response) and the distance from the

TABLE X

FIRST MEASURE OF GAIN AND SECOND MEASURE OF GAIN IN COMPLETION SENTENCES AND ARITHMETICAL PROBLEMS

Case No.	COMPLETION SENTENCES		ARITHMETICAL PROBLEMS	
	First Gain	Second Gain	First Gain	Second Gain
1	88	69	43	47
2	74	89	58	66
3	48	45	26	15
4	79	93	55	61
5	79	68	31	40
6	91	75	57	44
7	73	69	37	33
8	88	64	44	33
9	80	90	41	38
10	58	70	20	30
11	58	74	43	41
12	51	34	3	51
13	68	65	25	30
14	73	66	41	51
15	65	98	49	67
16	73	72	40	41
17	80	95	49	58
18	57	66	37	37
19	42	34	28	38
20	80	76	55	66
21	64	67	48	67
22	34	42	42	44
23	67	93	46	60
24	74	67	26	25
25	19	63	39	37
26	55	44	35	14
27	79	96	31	38
28	73	64	52	30
29	81	31	56	57
30	76	64	29	31
31	69	91	38	47
32	69	91	38	55
33	55	93	28	29
34	63	60	27	31
35	79	87	56	50
36	73	73	38	43
37	65	92	29	37
38	85	67	51	47
39	67	97	30	40
40	58	91	41	48
41	40	32	24	31
42	68	66	24	35
43	74	64	37	45
44	63	62	54	69
45	59	48	36	33

TABLE X (*Continued*)

| Case No. | COMPLETION SENTENCES | | ARITHMETICAL PROBLEMS | |
	First Gain	Second Gain	First Gain	Second Gain
46	47	62	33	39
47	89	94	24	39
48	58	59	26	29
49	44	55	40	32
50	66	95	47	49
51	48	51	20	30
52	37	36	28	27
53	41	49	20	32
54	69	88	50	48
55	86	98	53	57
56	55	46	34	41
57	83	81	60	73
58	66	79	48	56
59	90	81	50	48
60	69	85	28	44
61	64	44	26	54
62	76	89	37	43
63	61	97	44	44
64	62	56	28	30
65	56	70	46	54
66	71	92	53	56
67	69	82	52	63
68	91	96	52	52
69	91	97	52	65
70	54	65	31	36
71	59	64	43	40
72	92	93	28	41
73	62	66	28	52
74	57	85	39	58
75	73	64	67	53
76	84	87	60	39
77	63	67	28	36
78	45	70	44	30
79	53	63	41	51
80	60	64	26	29
81	77	95	40	47
82	68	70	54	56
83	47	48	49	35
84	68	77	42	48
85	51	55	44	24
86	64	53	28	17
87	81	91	42	51
88	74	93	29	42
89	80	81	46	32
90	43	58	24	32
91	74	72	25	29

TABLE X (*Concluded*)

Case No.	COMPLETION SENTENCES		ARITHMETICAL PROBLEMS	
	First Gain	Second Gain	First Gain	Second Gain
92	88	91	59	67
93	66	51	25	30
94	88	89	70	66
95	66	37	42	37
96	67	57	40	38
97	67	61	29	42

second to the nineteenth day (or the last day on which there was any correct response) will make equivalent gain scores. The number of practice periods will be seventeen periods. These two sets of initial and final scores are shown in Table X. The reliabilities of the gain scores of C and A are given in Table XI. The reliabilities thus obtained will be used to correct for attenuation the correlation between measures of tasks C and A and measures of intelligence. The correction of such correlations for attenuation will be difficult to interpret, for if we use the formula for attenuation it is necessary to have two independent series of measures for each function, but this dependence cannot be assumed where practice effects enter. Thus we

TABLE XI

RELIABILITY OF C AND A TASKS

Task	r	P.E.
Completion Sentences	.630	.0517
Arithmetical Problems	.644	.0400

are prevented in a very accurate attempt to correct the raw coefficient, but not to apply such a correction for attenuation is certain to minimize the value of the results. As the correlations become low or negative, the correction for attenuation becomes unsuitable. The raw correlations corrected for attenuation are here presented more for the purpose of contrasting correlations between intelligence tests than for the absolute accuracy of the attenuated correlations themselves. It is only by such an approximate comparison that we can estimate the true meaning of the raw correlations.

Since intelligence tests are the other variables in the correlations between intelligence scores and C and A scores, it is·also necessary to determine the reliabilities of these measures of intelligence. The reliability of Otis was determined by correlating scores on form A with scores on form B; the reliability of McCall was determined by correlating scores on two applications of the same form; the reliabilities of National A and B were determined by correlating scores on form 1 with scores on form 2; and the reliability of the combined tests was secured by correlating the first test scores combined with the second test scores combined. These reliabilities are recorded in Table XII. They range from .692 for the Otis to .830 for all of the tests combined. It must be remembered that the range of talent

TABLE XII

RELIABILITY OF INTELLIGENCE TESTS

Test	r	P.E.
Otis	.692	.0362
McCall	.801	.0249
National A	.800	.0249
National B	.792	.0260
National AB	.824	.0227
Combined	.830	.0216

for these tests is not the complete range of talent for which the tests were designed (approximately grades 3 to 8), as only children in grades 5, 6, and 7 took part in this experiment. With a narrower range of talent the reliability coefficients would not be as high as if children in grades 3 to 8 were used. Published reliabilities of these tests are based on the wider range of talent, but since their sigmas are not available there can be no comparison of such reliabilities by the formula

$$\frac{\sigma}{\Sigma} = \frac{\sqrt{1-R}}{\sqrt{1-r}}$$

The means and the sigmas of the intelligence tests scores are given in Table XIII.

The measures of validity that are practical within the limits

of this experiment are the intercorrelations of the intelligence
tests and the correlations of the intelligence tests with age.
These correlations with the corrections for attenuation (using
the reliabilities as given in Table XII with the exception of
the reliability of chronological age which, of course, is 1.00)
are given in Table XIV. These intercorrelations of intelligence
tests yield coefficients ranging from .674 (McCall with National
B) to .898 (Otis with National AB). The correlations of the
intelligence tests with chronological age are low, ranging from

TABLE XIII

MEAN AND SIGMA OF SCORES ON TWO FORMS OF THE
INTELLIGENCE TESTS

Test	Mean	Sigma
Otis A	45.78 ± 1.402*	13.67 ± .991*
Otis B	46.31 ± 1.281	12.62 ± .906
McCall 1st	53.23 ± .787	7.68 ± .557
McCall 2nd	54.26 ± .767	7.56 ± .550
National A-1	121.73 ± 2.103	20.54 ± 1.490
National A-2	122.25 ± 2.077	20.45 ± 1.468
National B-1	126.54 ± 2.114	20.82 ± 1.510
National B-2	126.84 ± 1.961	19.32 ± 1.388
National AB-1	248.27 ± 3.607	35.53 ± 2.550
National AB-2	249.09 ± 3.697	35.02 ± 2.515
Combined-1	49.62 ± 1.206	11.88 ± .852
Combined-2	50.68 ± 1.169	11.52 ± .827

* Standard error.

.153 (National A with age) to .239 (McCall with age). These
are about the correlations that would be expected with a range
of talent of three grades. The corrections for attenuation
show very high correlations in several cases, whereas the correlations between the McCall and the National AB do not
exceed .898. The sigma of chronological age is 13.23 ± .94 and
the mean is 141.61 ± 1.34 months.

With the reliabilities of the tasks C and A, the reliabilities of
the intelligence tests, and the validities of the intelligence tests
established, it is possible to describe adequately the relation
between intelligence and tasks C and A. The data describing

TABLE XIV

VALIDITY OF INTELLIGENCE TESTS

Tests Correlated	r	P.E.	Corrected for Attenuation
1. Otis and McCall	.749	.0299	1.008
2. Otis and National A	.722	.0329	.970
3. Otis and National B	.797	.0249	1.007
4. Otis and National AB	.898	.0134	1.192
5. McCall and National A	.719	.0331	.898
6. McCall and National B	.674	.0382	.867
7. McCall and National AB	.689	.0363	.862
8. National A and National B	.781	.0271	1.001
9. Otis and Age	.204	.0663	.245
10. McCall and Age	.239	.0652	.266
11. National A and Age	.153	.0675	.171
12. National B and Age	.204	.0663	.321
13. National AB and Age	.214	.0660	.234

the relationship between scores in tasks C and intelligence are presented in Table XV, and the data describing the relationship between scores in tasks A and intelligence are given in Table XVI. In each table the correlations corrected for attenuation are only those whose reliabilities are previously given. The first six items in each table show the relationship between the initial scores and measures of intelligence, the next six items (numbered 7 to 12) show the relationship between final scores and measures of intelligence, the next six items (numbered 13 to 18) show the relationship between gross gains and measures of intelligence, and the last six items (numbered 19 to 24) show the relationship between per cent gains and the measures of intelligence.

The correlations between intelligence and tests C and A are, in general, almost as high as the validities of the intelligence tests themselves and when corrected for attenuation they are in many cases higher than the raw correlations between the intelligence tests, but not higher than the attenuated correlations. In two cases the correlations of tasks C and A with intelligence are higher than the coefficient of validity for the intelligence tests, for in tasks A the final scores correlate with intelligence Otis .699 ± .0350, and intelligence tests combined

.746 ± .0304, while the McCall and National AB correlate only
.689 ± .0363. The differences are not significant: the ratios of
the difference to the probable error of the difference being respectively 1.212 and .198). In tasks C the final scores and
intelligence tests combined correlate .658 ± .0401 and this is almost as high as the correlation of McCall with National AB

TABLE XV

RELATION BETWEEN SCORES ON COMPLETION SENTENCES AND ON
INTELLIGENCE TESTS

Score and Test Correlated	r	P.E.	Corrected for Attenuation
1. Initial Score and Otis	.440	.0558	
2. Initial Score and McCall	.523	.0503	
3. Initial Score and National A	.538	.0485	
4. Initial Score and National B	.325	.0623	
5. Initial Score and National AB	.459	.0546	
6. Initial Score and Combined	.367	.0597	
7. Final Score and Otis	.615	.0422	
8. Final Score and McCall	.628	.0417	
9. Final Score and National A	.575	.0471	
10. Final Score and National B	.519	.0506	
11. Final Score and National AB	.611	.0434	
12. Final Score and Combined	.658	.0401	
13. Gain and Otis	.667	.0377	1.012
14. Gain and McCall	.553	.0483	.779
15. Gain and National A	.596	.0447	.840
16. Gain and National B	.453	.0553	.642
17. Gain and National AB	.524	.0497	.729
18. Gain and Combined	.591	.0451	.809
19. Per Cent Gain and Otis	.555	.0487	
20. Per Cent Gain and McCall	.503	.0520	
21. Per Cent Gain and National A	.451	.0564	
22. Per Cent Gain and National B	.396	.0586	
23. Per Cent Gain and National AB	.448	.0552	
24. Per Cent Gain and Combined	.514	.0513	

(.689 ± .0363). The difference is not significant (the ratio is
.555). In fact, the correlation between intelligence tests combined and the final scores in tasks A (.746 ± .0304) is higher
than the correlation between Otis and National A (.722 ±
.0329), McCall and National A (.719 ± .0331), McCall and
National B (.674 ± .0382), and McCall and National AB
(.689 ± .0363). None of these differences is significant (ratios

are respectively .528, .600, 1.445, and 1.212). The highest correlation between gains and intelligence is the C gains with Otis, which is .667 ± .0377, and the second highest correlation is the A gains with intelligence tests combined, which is .620 ± .0426, while the lowest correlation between intelligence tests is McCall and National B, .674 ± .0382. The differences are not significant (ratios are .130 and .769 respectively). The highest cor-

TABLE XVI

RELATION BETWEEN SCORES OF ARITHMETICAL PROBLEMS AND ON
INTELLIGENCE TESTS

Score and Test Correlated	r	P.E.	Correction for Attenuation
1. Initial Score and Otis	.349	.0605	
2. Initial Score and McCall	.308	.0621	
3. Initial Score and National A	.305	.0621	
4. Initial Score and National B	.242	.0648	
5. Initial Score and National AB	.206	.0662	
6. Initial Score and Combined	.390	.0589	
7. Final Score and Otis	.699	.0350	
8. Final Score and McCall	.602	.0438	
9. Final Score and National A	.597	.0445	
10. Final Score and National B	.529	.0498	
11. Final Score and National AB	.446	.0555	
12. Final Score and Combined	.746	.0304	
13. Gain and Otis	.599	.0442	.951
14. Gain and McCall	.555	.0476	.776
15. Gain and National A	.542	.0486	.758
16. Gain and National B	.468	.0540	.658
17. Gain and National AB	.539	.0610	.542
18. Gain and Combined	.620	.0426	.848
19. Per Cent Gain and Otis	.575	.0464	
20. Per Cent Gain and McCall	.528	.0497	
21. Per Cent Gain and National A	.567	.0466	
22. Per Cent Gain and National B	.405	.0581	
23. Per Cent Gain and National AB	.489	.0527	
24. Per Cent Gain and Combined	.553	.0478	

relation between per cent gains and intelligence is per cent gains in tasks A with Otis, which is .575 ± .0464; the second highest correlation is per cent gains in tasks A with National A, which is .567 ± .0466. Comparing these with the lowest correlation between intelligence tests, which is McCall and National B (.674 ± .0382), the ratios of the difference of the means to the probable error of the difference are 1.650 and 1.783 respectively.   In none of the above are the differences in the correlations between measures of tasks C and A and intelligence and the correlations between intelligence tests themselves statistically significant.   From the correlations corrected for attenuation it is seen that if we had perfectly reliable measures of tasks C and A and perfectly reliable measures of intelligence, these would correlate practically as high as measures of intelligence would correlate with themselves.

The only other measurable factor we have that can affect the relationship between scores in tasks C and A and intelligence is age.   Partial correlations with age held constant are presented

TABLE XVII

PARTIAL CORRELATION BETWEEN GAIN SCORES ON TASK C AND INTELLIGENCE SCORES AND BETWEEN GAIN SCORES ON TASK A AND INTELLIGENCE SCORES WHEN AGE IS HELD CONSTANT

Measures Correlated	Partial r	P.E.
1. Gain in C and Otis	.672	.0381
2. Gain in C and McCall	.557	.0475
3. Gain in C and National A	.596	.0443
4. Gain in C and National B	.453	.0552
5. Gain in C and National AB	.523	.0500
6. Gain in C and Combined	.591	.0454
7. Gain in A and Otis	.591	.0454
8. Gain in A and McCall	.533	.0497
9. Gain in A and National A	.456	.0550
10. Gain in A and National B	.463	.0544
11. Gain in A and National AB	.536	.0492
12. Gain in A and Combined	.723	.0333

in Table XVII.   Since the correlations between tasks C and A and age are low and the correlations between measures of intelligence and age are also low, these partial correlations vary little from the correlations of zero order, and age is not a serious factor in the relationships.

These correlations, especially the correlations of final scores with intelligence, are very similar to the correlations found by Clark ['25] and quoted by Thorndike ['26, p. 97 and p. 107] between stock intelligence examinations and level scores in arithmetical problems and sentence completions.   Clark's correlations vary from a correlation of .74 between arithmetic level and the Otis Self-Administering Tests to .55 between completion level and the Otis test. If both variables were perfect measures these correlations would be .83 and .61 respectively. The correlations in the present study are somewhat higher and yet the number of cases is relatively small, only 97 subjects. These correlations are comparatively high for a single mental function with a composite of mental functions, as represented in general intelligence tests.

We may conclude that the type of scores in tasks C and A that are obtained by the plan of the learning experiments herein described are closely related to intelligence as measured by the stock intelligence test, and that completion sentences and arithmetical problems are each reliable units for the measurement of intelligence.

CHAPTER V

CONCLUSIONS

SINCE the conclusions of this experiment must be viewed in the light of the distinctive nature of the materials involved, a brief survey will be made of the problem in its setting. The use of completion sentences and arithmetical problems as types of mental functions in intelligence tests has been widely accepted. The completion sentence has been used from the time of Ebbinghaus [1897] to Thorndike ['26], and arithmetical problems are found in many general intelligence tests. These two types of problems or mental tasks are the C and A in the well known CAVD Intelligence Tests of Thorndike. A number of different kinds of arithmetic problems used in intelligence tests, including the CAVD Intelligence Tests, are taught in school. Completion exercises, as such, are seldom taught in school, although some questions asked by teachers and certain exercises in language and grammar take the form of sentence completion.

The general plan of learning experiments reviewed by Kincaid ['25] and others, in which the practice exercise is employed, offers a method for studying the sentence completion and arithmetical problem solving functions. However, a review of these studies shows the absence of an absolute zero and, therefore, the presence of a statistical error in all measures of gain and per cent gain. The Thorndike C and A tasks have difficulty values based on an absolute zero and, therefore, if used as tasks to be solved will give scores without these errors. Gross gains will be true gains and ratios of gains with initial scores will be true ratios. Further, these tasks represent higher and more nearly pure mental functions than those employed in previous experiments in which the tasks were more simple. The previous experiments measured the ability to do the same kinds of

44

things better and faster rather than solve problems or complete sentences with changing content involving organization and reasoning. These C and A tasks were arranged in order of difficulty and presented to subjects for nineteen experimental periods. A mean initial score, a mean final score, a mean gain, and a mean per cent gain for each subject in tasks C and A furnish the essential primary data for studying these functions as elements for measuring intelligence.

The data point clearly to the influence of intelligence as affecting the final scores. Measures of absolute and relative variability show much greater variability in final scores than in initial scores. The ratios of the worse and better records also show an increase in variability from initial scores to final scores. Subjects who made high initial scores made high final scores and gained more than subjects who made low initial scores; and the differences are statistically significant. Bright subjects, when brightness is determined by general intelligence tests, made higher final scores and made greater gains than duller subjects; and the differences are statistically significant in six out of ten cases. In the remaining four cases the differences are always in favor of the brighter group.

A study of the relationship between general intelligence tests scores and mean initial scores, mean final scores, mean gross gains, and mean per cent gains shows low but positive correlation for mean initial scores and fair to high correlations for final scores, gross gains, and per cent gains. In a few cases, especially in the correlations with final scores, the correlations are as high as several of the correlations between some of the general intelligence tests. Known reliabilities of the general intelligence tests and reliabilities of gain scores permitted the correction of raw correlations for attenuation. A few of these were perfect and all were high, especially in the case of final scores. Age was not a factor in any of these relationships, for the partial correlations with age held constant vary little from the correlations of zero order. These correlations indicate that the scores in tasks C and A are due in a large measure to intelligence and therefore are measures of intelligence. It is really interesting to find a measure of a single function, such as completion or problem solving, correlating so highly with measures of a composite of a number of functions as are represented by the general intelligence tests used. Such functions, therefore, are extremely valuable as units in intelligence tests and should occupy a large and important part of all the different types of functions used in measurements of intelligence.

BIBLIOGRAPHY

Binet, A. "Attention and Adaptation." *L'Annee Psychologigue,* 1899, Vol. VI, pp. 248-404.

Chapman, J. C. *Individual Differences in Ability and Improvement and Their Correlations.* Contributions to Education, No. 63. Teachers College, Columbia University, 1914.

Chapman, J. C. "Statistical Considerations in Interpreting the Effect of Training on Individual Differences." *Psychological Review,* 1925, Vol. XXXII, pp. 224-234.

Clark, J. R. *The Relation of Speed, Range, and Level to Score on Intelligence Tests.* 1925.

Division of Psychology, Institute of Educational Research, *The I.E.R. Inventory of Intellectual Tasks and Their Difficulty.* Teachers College, Columbia University, 1926 (Mimeographed Edition).

Ebbinghaus, Hermann. "Ueber eine neue Methode zur Prufung geistiger Fahigkeiten und ihre Anwendung bei Schulkindern," *Zeitschrift für Psychologie,* Vol. 13, 1897, pp. 401-459.

Garrett, Henry E. "A Study of the CAVD Intelligence Examination." *Journal of Educational Research,* 1930, Vol. XXIV, pp. 103-109.

Gates, Arthur I. "The Nature and Limit of Improvement Due to Training." *Twenty-seventh Yearbook,* Part I, National Society for the Study of Education, 1928, pp. 441-460.

Hollingworth, H. L. "Individual Differences Before, During, and After Practice." *Psychological Review,* 1914, Vol. XXI, pp. 1-8.

Holzinger, Karl J. "Thorndike's C.A.V.D. Is Full of G." *Journal of Educational Psychology,* 1931, Vol. XXII, pp. 161-166.

Hull, Clark. "The Conversion of Test Scores into Series Which Shall Have Any Assigned Mean and Degree of Dispersion." *Journal of Applied Psychology,* 1922, p. 299.

Hunsicker, Lillian May. *A Study of the Relationship Between Rate and Ability.* Contributions to Education, No. 185. Teachers College, Columbia University, 1925.

Johnson, B. "Practice Effects in a Target Test, A Comparative Study of Groups Varying in Intelligence." *Psychological Review,* 1919, Vol. XXVI, pp. 300-316.

Kelley, Truman L. *Educational Guidance.* Contributions to Education, No. 71. Teachers College, Columbia University, 1914.

Kincaid, M. "Individual Differences in Learning." *Psychological Review,* 1925, Vol. XXXII, pp. 34-53.

Lorge, Irving. *Influence of Regularly Interpolated Time Intervals Upon Subsequent Learning.* Contributions to Education, No. 138. Teachers College, Columbia University, 1930.

McCall, W. A. *How to Experiment in Education.* Macmillan, 1923.

National Research Council, *Conference on Individual Psychological Differences.* Washington, D. C., 1930.

Ordahl, L. E. and Ordahl, G. "Qualitative Differences Between Levels of Intelligence in Feeble-Minded Children." *Journal of Psycho-Asthenics,* 1915, Monograph Supplement, Vol. I, pp. 1-50.

Peterson, Joseph. "Johnson's Measurement of Rate of Improvement Under Practice." *Journal of Educational Psychology,* 1924, Vol. XV, pp. 271-275.

Race, Henrietta V. *Improvability, Its Correlations and Its Relations to Initial Ability.* Contributions to Education, No. 124. 1922. Teachers College, Columbia University.

Reed, H. B. "The Effect of Training on Individual Differences." *Journal of Experimental Psychology,* 1924, Vol. VII, pp. 186-200.

Ruch, Giles M. "Influence of the Factor of Intelligence on the Form of the Learning Curve." *Psychological Monographs,* 1925, Vol. 34, No. 7, pp. 1-64.

Spearman, C. and Krueger, F. "Die Korrelation zwischen Verschiedenen Geistigen Leistungsfahigkeiten." *Zeitschrift für Psychologie,* 1907, Vol. XLIV, pp. 50-114.

Stoddard, George D. "Individual Differences in Learning." *Psychological Review,* 1925, Vol. XXXII, pp. 479-485.

Thomson, Godfrey H. "A Formula to Correct the Effect of Errors of Measures on the Correlation of Initial Values With Gains." *Journal of Experimental Psychology,* 1924, Vol. VII, pp. 321-324.

Thorndike, E. L. *Mental and Social Measurement.* Teachers College, Columbia University, 1904.

Thorndike, E. L. "The Effect of Practice in the Case of a Purely

Intellectual Function." *American Journal of Psychology,* 1908, Vol. XIX, pp. 374-384.

Thorndike, E. L. *Educational Psychology,* Vol. III, Bureau of Publications, Teachers College, Columbia University, 1914.

Thorndike, E. L. *The Measurement of Intelligence.* Bureau of Publications, Teachers College, Columbia University, 1926.

Thorndike, E. L. "The Influence of the Chance Imperfections of Measures upon the Relation of Initial Score to Gain or Loss." *Journal of Experimental Psychology,* 1924, Vol. VII, pp. 225-232.

Wilson, Frank T. *Learning of Bright and Dull Children.* Contributions to Education, No. 292. Teachers College, Columbia University, 1928.

Yule, G. Udny. *An Introduction to the Theory of Statistics.* Charles Griffin and Company, Ltd., 1924.